DECLARATIONS OF HUNGER

POEMS

REED SMITH

DECLARATIONS OF HUNGER

POEMS
REED SMITH

BROOKLYN ARTS PRESS * LOS ANGELES

Declarations of Hunger
© 2025 Reed Smith

ISBN-13: 978-1-936767-60-1

Cover design by Alban Fischer.

Edited by Joe Pan.

All rights reserved. No part of this publication may be reproduced by any means existing or to be developed in the future without written consent by the publisher.

Published in the United States of America by:
Brooklyn Arts Press
www.BrooklynArtsPress.com
info@BrooklynArtsPress.com

Distributed to the trade by Asterism Books and Ingram.

Library of Congress Cataloging-in-Publication Data

Names: Smith, Reed, author.
Title: Declarations of hunger : poems / Reed Smith.
Other titles: Declarations of hunger (Compilation)
Description: First edition. | Los Angeles : Brooklyn Arts Press, 2025. | Summary: "Debut collection of poetry by Reed Smith"-- Provided by publisher.
Identifiers: LCCN 2024045370 | ISBN 9781936767601 (paperback)
Subjects: LCGFT: Poetry.
Classification: LCC PS3619.M5924626 D43 2025 | DDC 811/.6--dc23/eng/20241007
LC record available at https://lccn.loc.gov/2024045370

FIRST EDITION

for Kristy

and for Gabby & Charley

CONTENTS

RIVER OF LOVE	11
THE EVIDENCE AT HAND	12
THE VOICES OF THE MIND	14
FALL IN THE CONEJOS	15
RECURRENCES	16
DECLARATIONS OF HUNGER	18
COYOTES	19
PEAU D'ORANGE	20
JACK'S HOUSE	21
EMBOUCHURE	22
HOW DEEP IS THE OCEAN?	24
THE SOUND OF APPROACHING SILENCE	25
GRAFFITI	26
STONE FIGURES	27
BIRTHDAY REMINDER FOR THE DEAD	28
PASSING IT	30
MESSAGE IN A BOTTLE	31
CLASSIC MAN	33
MEAT MARKET	34
THE STORY OF YOUR BIRTH	37
REFLECTIONS	40

GOLDEN HOUR	42
FATHER'S DAY	44
SAGE ON THE NORTH PLATTE	45
RESUSCITATION	46
CHALLENGER	48
A TIME OF PLENTY	49
FIDDLERS	51
ENTRE RIOS	52
BIRDS OF PARADISE	53
TREE OF ONE	55
FAMILIAR BANDAGES	56
EASTER, EL SARGENTO	57
LIFE GOES ON	58
GIRL BURNING	60
BOWL OF APPLES	61
SENSE OF TIME	62
HOME SCHOOL	63
ACKNOWLEDGMENTS	66
AUTHOR BIO	67

DECLARATIONS OF HUNGER

POEMS

REED SMITH

RIVER OF LOVE

The river of love is unsuited to loving well.
In one, it traps and drowns a man
trying to learn how to swim. It pulls him
down like a bucket on a rope,

a greedy lens of current going past.
Its efficiency is astonishing. Nothing
ever really ends up given back.
It repeats the curse. It traps the orgasm.

Annoyed with the field, it cuts
the field in half. It unlocks stones
that have no keyhole. Drink its water
and the universe expands invisibly

inside you. Rubble of cold stars.
A heart of Mars glass. If you cross it
you can count yourself as changed.
A toe goes in; a shell or husk returns.

THE EVIDENCE AT HAND

They drove east out of the borrowed city.
To find jobs. To start new lives.
Somewhere along the way they killed
a young couple traveling the country.

They burned their van. They murdered
a botanist. His "gentle soul" bloomed
to ash. As for their own bodies,
their special treatment was no less

loathsome. Self-inflicted gunshots
in a marsh near Gillam, Manitoba.
On TV, I listen to what their mothers say.
The grief of the killer's families

strikes me like cold rain. They have
stepped into nothing they paid for
but own it just the same. They are
somber, pale, waxy as the dead,

but you can see their anger like dirty
light leaking through a painted bulb.
Later, at home, they find it all over
again. The town will talk

like it always does. It takes night
to silence the rumor mill churning
its clattering belts. A long darkness,
the kind that constricts, choking out

the trees, the cold smoke, the snow
on the frozen streets. It winds out
in webs, four corners, farther even,
to where evidence is no longer

something that proves any facts,
like a poem about the way the world
works, or these words, these
words,
          these words.

THE VOICES OF THE MIND

They ambush a door left open,
a black felt hat tossed on a bed.
They remind you they made a point
of saying *enjoy it while you can.*

And also:
You are not that important. It is not always about you.

They pause while you take a breath, a whole
troop of unreadable selves
carrying their subjects to the fire.

I'd like to think that even in your worst way,
you are true to them. The words you say
jibe with actions committed,
                                      the *Shit!* you curse
with that you step in,
proving you no liar, good or bad.

Like a trick of the light, they surprise you.
They call it love. You try to mean it.

FALL IN THE CONEJOS

Iron gives way to salt.
Great lakes of it burn the sky
with its mirrors.

The river fragments into an academy
of eyes. Grass blurs in the sulfur-bog.
Shivering willows blaze
the last yellows of October.
Cattle pass in burlap shadow.

Mushrooms rise from manure,
lifting the desiccated fecal discs.
Their gills are clotted in the
currant jelly of frozen gypsum.
They are veined like marble,
edges dimmed to a pale half-glow.

The smell of blood. High vapor,
dark pines. Frost on granite.
Leaf harem of roseate confetti.
A great mass of division
below the feet. Fractals of dark
plates forcing the land apart.

Clouds loosely bandaged in the sky.
The shock of the cold—a handful
of nails. Resinous river
with useful tools that pull
and push, battering rocks
when the snow melts,
winnowed down to wizened crusts,
strange codes, geometric shadows.

RECURRENCES

September sunlight scattered on rotting
gourds picked over by a raven
who visits every fall carrying with him a dusting
of coal ash from the city.

~

Rushmore. The Moorish Lions. Bolivar's dreams.
Mica schist, fine-veined granite.
Water wrinkles faces in the fountains.
Terminal bodies of tin cans tremble on electrodes of sunlight.

~

The living flatter the dead. They ease them down,
empty their pockets. A girl with no clothes
runs naked down a road. A boy whose head is scorched
and bloody sits patiently, hair matted in brick dust.

~

I try not to listen to the woman who tells
her daughter, "Don't be afraid, let's pray,"
as naturally as if rising from sleep.
The airplane's fuselage pitted with noise like a gourd-rattle.

~

Bolivar's dreams rose from the Century of Lights—
cold shards of ruined light eaten
like moons of scoured ash. Lunar moths in the porchlight
flutter over squashes rotting in our garden.

DECLARATIONS OF HUNGER
after A. E. Backus

He paints a bird and a snake.
                              It is midday
in a field. One glistens cruelly. One tries not
to give itself away.

The fractal swath of deliverance
glitters in the ocean's current.

Wind hammers inside the echo chamber's hood.

Wings, like dusty Sanskrit, blur.

They tangle in a whisper.
A heron becomes a wren. A rock becomes a weed.
The grass shakes its sequined blades.

Declarations of hunger have been made.

COYOTES

Early barks like rifle shots slapping
flatwater. A kinned pack hunting.
Arroyo unaffiliated with the grade

gathering its moraine shadows
before dawn, slabs of pursed
pinons prospecting western distances,

all for water, the ware
of the next century. Suddenly it ends.
Talking becomes familiar again.

The killing grounds lifted back
to the sun's tradition.
Horizon combed neatly by fire.

The lineman's generator kicks
up blue exhaust, shivering eels
slippery as grease.

The demented housecat
comes back slopped in loose dust.
New choirs start preternaturally.

PEAU D'ORANGE

She survived what inflation did
in the 30's to those families
with one car, no gas money, no jobs.
Her sister ran off with a fraud.
Her father shot squirrels in the yard.
He did telegraphy for the railroad.
In Fiji, a woman's body turned up.
Colorado Springs had three that year.
All other people's daughters.
She stopped looking, rode down
to Dallas on the Texas Eagle.
Imported names of barons
on the ivy-laced street signs.
Looking back, she was shrewd
by upper middle-class standards.
She ate two small meals a day.
Skipped lunch for the sacrament
of menthol smoke. Crystalized
the lungs, her doctors said,
ate her from the inside out.
Their work-a-day words
pulled from ancient Latin,
sometimes French.
Their offices swam in a thin,
blue haze. Ashtrays
and magazines conjured order
in the fever-choked waiting room,
where death filtered in
as sunlight under the door.

JACK'S HOUSE

The closets stink of termite chaff.
Cockroach malt. Sunlight's lacy patterns

stain the plaster's castrated hide.

Folios of seeds folded tight in paper beaks.
Dust tames the pitch of the funeral bowlers.

It's half slapdash, squatting on syphilitic

pier and beam, quivering on haunches
rotting through after years of nights

where stars tested exposure without

the means of light. Powdered lime
bruises the petrified Okies sleeping

under the marigolds. The last century is

canned fresh. Catfish glitter in the black
pond. Nitrate's cold laureates struggle

to breathe. The children don't come back.

Ruin streams in. The once-fallow cornfields
chopped into dead quarters.

Slaughter seeps into the skin.

EMBOUCHURE

after Chet Baker

New Year's Day. Frost ruffles
the dirty pages of the field.
A milk-blue flux clings to the
wilting lashes of corn stubble.

The landlord clears the road.
His tractor bogs on the hill, coughs up
dregs of burnt oil. He walks down,
makes the highway and is gone.

We listen to *Fair Weather*.
Wind meanders over the rows.
We talk in the bowels of the house.
The water lines knock and seize.

His father bought the farm years ago.
He cobbled miscreant vegetables
from the endless pastures of lime
the summer cars here spatter

with their all-purpose Goodyears.
His son married a younger woman
when his first wife died.
She came from Cedar Rapids.

She played an old French horn.
You could hear how awful she was
from the hill up the road. In spring,
snowmelt flooded the fields.

The soy rotted on its stalks.
Summer turned the ragged bolls
into wind-trembled stomas.
He loved to talk about false doors,

cellars of crushed diatoms.
His father had been a banker.
There had been no misplaced tradition.
He loved both his wives. The first

was unlucky. She died of cancer
the year wind split our field in two.
Groundhogs climbed the banked
mounds of snow to stretch

and ruminate. His next wife outlived him.
She row-planted daisies in the
front yard that resembled graves.
She kept the windows sealed in summer.

Alive together, she'd ride the middle
seat of the truck beside him.
They'd park in the pasture,
flip the lights. August dusk a Persian

carpet. The light a refugee
of past lights. No less beautiful,
they'd wait till it all died.
He'd slide over and she would drive.

HOW DEEP IS THE OCEAN?

In the mirror undressing
  I see what you see

I shut the doors to the room
    I cannot ask the question
I always asked before

To anyone else I emit no signal
   but to you
                    my crooked stations
are what live alone
creaking in the wavy corners
of the night

My trajectory hasn't changed

In the crook of the tree's
elbow in the
life-span of a wingbeat

Two known worlds cradle my head

They let me sleep
murmuring
only the occasional pejorative

Elysian snow

THE SOUND OF APPROACHING SILENCE

Gray wood ziggurat with bell and cross,
petals in nova, tiny mounds no bigger

than shoeboxes—a cemetery for children.
In the vapor of morning we hike the

bottom land, down through flaccid bull
nettle, damp grass, to new beginnings

of the stream. We leave the mortal
poverty behind. Daddy's little thing

won't get up and follow since the shovels
put her down. Red ants labor there now.

Weeds listen, ambush boots at the gate.
The sky blushes creosote. Wind turns

aside the shrieks of ravens in the trees.
The storm is still in the trough of silence,

far away, quiet as a satellite returning
its data, greeting us with its flickering lights.

GRAFFITI

The Pharaohs didn't
forget it in their graves—
their tombs blazed
with bony stenciled wings
and vague, muscled
implements. They knew
its uses: need a citizen
dead and the bloody O
of the setting sun slid
like yolk onto his hut's
plastered door. His daughter,
with a look of varnished
guilt, led him out
like a blind mole
the next morning.
What power. One brushstroke.
A swipe of fizz.
Now these patterns
rise within earshot
of strip malls & ballparks,
on the fence
behind my house,
the bathroom
at the nursing home.
Passing slowly
on the steel shanks
of boxcars as the sun sets
from Seattle to Ocala,
I look for my name:
where it came from,
where it goes.

STONE FIGURES

–Sans-Soucis Palace, Haiti

Afternoons walking sun-bleached
orchards. Clouds lurch past on fire.
The statues are Henri Christophe's.
Alabaster urns, fragmented spheres,
a marble angel who looks down a hill
toward the gravel hum of generators
by the stream in the village. The sea
glints on its wheel in the distance.
Ash from the cooking fires clots
like chicken fat in the welds of the
broken stairs. The angel keeps
a record of her daily torture. Ash drips
from the wounds on her wings.
A silver bullet took Henri's life.
The silver sun hangs like a prayer
or a motive above us, its intention
not completely unknown.

BIRTHDAY REMINDER FOR THE DEAD

Arrives on a Monday.

                In a hand holding
a firecracker, a razor, a lacerating shank of glass.

The mailman won't leave it in the box.
        Tosses it in the carport.

Lizards, ants. Don't linger. Move on.

Passed between so many hands the words
flow over it like water. Waves.

Beware, or because?

You jump to the end.

Even the cat could take a clue. Wandered off
to die. Refused to be found.

Postcard, or appointment?

Each word a time-stamp. You jump to the end.

So precious. Belongs only to you.
Signature is yours. Postage not enough.

Return to sender.

Sincerely yours.

Couldn't take a clue.
Sent back.

Needed a reminder.

Arrived on a Monday.

PASSING IT

On the far side of the blue field
evening settles below a scrim of smoke
like the lid of a pot being lifted.
The flitting swish of the grubby grass
interrupts the rumor of the turn
toward fall, the neat staking-down
and twining-up of the fat harvest.
Driving home in dusk, leaning
into the night ahead.

A marsh hawk squats
on a fencepost, keening for voles
in the wind-spilled chaff. Its eyes
catch the headlights: dull, blood-
yellow yolks, savage torches.
Early starlight crackles on spears of grass
snapped off in the sky's blackened shield.
A sudden lisp of rain drives
the hawk into the trees. It dives
low, gliding on a trance of wind,
wing feathers copper with raindrops,
talons pulled in as it swoops.

MESSAGE IN A BOTTLE

A message in a bottle was tossed off the side of a German ship on June 12, 1886, as it sailed through the Indian Ocean, the date and location penned carefully in script on the scroll inside.

-New York Times, *March 7, 2018*

131 years later, it's still about the currents
and where they take you.
Two lifetimes. Too many wars to count.

It is the stuff of legend. Of omen.
The person who finds it cautiously
celebrates. It takes months to become

forgotten again. It was just like
the Germans to date, sign, and plot
its location in perfectly-written script.

There could be no confusing
what it meant. A love poem would
have served better. A letter of regret

scribbled on the Indian Ocean
to a father dying in Hamburg.
With no way to post or deliver it.

Because the words are anyone's,
it carries only circumstance.
Useful data that would help cargo

arrive faster in Perth. The unblinking
terminals wait. Premature lines
drawn through paper oceans,

waves glisten and tumble.
The engineer is leaning far out
over the balcony, thinking forward

to who will find it, and where.
There is no other option.
Preparations are underway.

CLASSIC MAN

Give them an inch they take a mile.
Squirming in the shadows.
Scraping cornstalks to the bone.
Crows. One lands, then more
slicken the black plate of field.

I'm weak. I shake a leg but never
move from this spot. I stand
at the window watching myself.
Husk and linen, thinly skinned.
The pipe that doesn't smoke.

Soil cribs against me and fall
slackens clods. The tractors ferment
rows of sour vowels. The landlord
forgets his axe. I sleep in the gradual
ease of corn-nest, fingers gouged

to whispers. They've eaten even
me. Sometimes you wake up alive
in the real world. Origins lisp.
A dog turns you to piss. The reverence
you once felt outstares you.

MEAT MARKET

It was the dirty years,
a dirty life
we led back then,

a string of thoughts
telling us where we *could*
have been.

The out-of-state
geese set up impromptu
shows in the fields.

Sundays, the Chevy
chugged inelegant miles
through cattle pastures

toward La Grange.
There was a meat market
of red brick on the square.

It was an obstacle course
of ground beef
and cut pink lungs

ringed by the chiseled
piping of Easter grass.
Yards of marbled steak,

pigs feet flipped skyward,
iridescent knuckled toes;
peppered backs of bacon shanks

blotted to protect a stubbled glaze.
The leaded windows
sealed tightly

with yellow newspapers
brittle as dried zebra skin.
The butchers were brothers.

Boxers with stone hands,
inlander brutes
who saved my mother

the best tenderloin.
The truth always makes a curve.
Their voices, viscera

attenuated in its wet slough,
the damp chalk of brick,
the heat outside

a muzzle of warm breath.
I saw it again last year.
There is a billboard outside

that says *Believe!*
A man hosed the steps
with a pulse of cloudy water.

The water crawled over
the hot cement. It hissed
like the herald tongue

of a rising flood.
It lapped at my feet, against
the glacier blue windows.

It split apart, split again,
a divided rubble
of greasy foam,

bits of meat in reverse
canter. The leavings,
sometimes done up

in a pressed loaf,
sometimes washed
away in the gutter.

THE STORY OF YOUR BIRTH

Gaff and arrow, I think
of them now when the
metal tools clink against

the conveyor's teeth steaming
and clean, your unfenced
weight not yet a true loaf

tethered to your
mother inside.
Strangers picked

the locks in their tongues
to wager your sex
but all I could hear

was a fool's interpretation
of the book of fatherhood,
its echoes of grief,

of tenderness, the words (not yours)
glutting my ears with salt.
I gave a lot of thought to it—

now that I was bulled
and disappearing—
how you would be

a refugee
to a cherished anatomy,
something winged

and sliced in two
at the same time,
twilit from the beginning,

a native whitewashed
dismissal. God help me
I rehearsed this.

A compulsive waker,
I reached out of a dream
for any real name

with a smell or a taste.
Unsound, blanched,
indecent,

the clouds unreeled
untroubled. The Healers
encouraged her to walk.

Oak trees
speckled with snow,
each tiny white aphid

a canopy of your mother's
curd. All night,
through the next day.

Sawdust mute
where it settled.
Pale flames

in the Cyclops' eye.
I told an officer
who listened to the

sedentary reports
on the radio I was surprised
at what my money

did not buy. He sat
at the end
of nothing, one boot up

crowding his knee,
a composite of the body
that had been mine,

down to the casual
membrane put up
between us,

its own fabulous
dismissal prophesied—
pride, he said

that sounds almost like pride.

REFLECTIONS

I have an hour to myself today
    to disorder the familiar.
It's what I do now when
        I can't remember
how I got here,
    when the newly-wrinkled face
        stops to stare at me
in windows, coffee cups, ponds, puddles—
surprised it's been noticed
    at all. The rubble of words
        jerks
    like paper in a fire.
The sky is black milk behind the clouds, a blood-
      stain dampening
          the sand. It is hot.
    Morning never
        brings much
           respite. Venus
    has tipped her blue eye into view
as if
out of contempt for Mars.
      Higher
    up, tiny and red,
      the God
shimmers in the night's last wind. All at
    once and nothing is the model
      of planetary
    happenstance. Here and gone.
        But their flight
    is made already,
mapped from one
        end of the sky to the other.

                Next year,
    at the same time, they will turn up
                        the sleeping
            birds who never
sang their despair. They'll glare at one
                    another, goddess and warrior,
        remembering what it was like
to find themselves
            in this same sky
                            being watched
                in the raw early summer
before the sun came up
                            and burned them
            off the face of the earth.

GOLDEN HOUR

The sun has set not long ago,
a fiery unravelling in the
book my daughters
fight over. A silly phalanx
of goofy-looking animals
brushing fangs and tusks,
taking baths, descending
below decks to gamble
their luck with sleep.

Charlotte likes the pig best.
His snout is a slab of pink,
its white bone-in center,
nostrils like glossy marbles.
His tail swishes pertly inside
his frumpy blue pajamas.

The boat they are on is a tipsy
iron coffin rocking
on ugly sawtooth waves.
The animals seem oblivious
that there is no captain.
The boat drifts on its own.

They go down, one by one—
hooves, flippers, bear paws.
The ark is almost full by now.
We read it again, watch them
make their choice, to stay or go,
thinking how nice
the moon looks, how warm
the salt air must be.

But it is time.
The pig leads the way.
The night is long. The sea
is deep. They rock and rock
and rock to sleep.

FATHER'S DAY

One last time, I am a hero.
I can do no wrong. I'm hailed for
little more than paying attention.
It's like a game in which I do nothing,
and still win. I open gifts, eat
strawberry cake. But when I grow
nostalgic, and give my kids something
that once meant the world to me,
it is changed in their peculiar view
of possession. In this house, it is
easy come, easy go. Gold would be
passed over for cardboard.
I want them to know that we live
with pieces of the dead, relics
that keep us clear of emptiness
and dread by the simplest
connections. That blood only goes
so far, but that contained, it is not
invisible, and sets us to work
with its ethic, mending, perfecting
our progress as we stitch up
the rough patterns we've created.

SAGE ON THE NORTH PLATTE

Uncorrupted blankets of sage
spattered with dusty raindrops.
Placid menthol, damp tidal pitch
rising out of the bosque loam,
the true-born color-in-the-mouth
of fractal cloud and faraway sky,
lavender kindled purple for the bees,
flooded with the hum of a thousand wings.
The river is dull, brown. White caps
like troweled aprons rising, falling,
unseen current tugging, smoothing them.
You behind, far enough you are years
younger, quiet in concentration, indelible.
The pastel hills. A lunette-shaped lisp
of rain grazes the thirsty valley.
All of it confuses some other time
when the sheets submit to charity.
When everything is given away
to make room for more inventory.
That's you in a field of scrubby sage.
The wind is wet, darkening the leaves.
Inept memories. Pictures without
colors true to their stories.

RESUSCITATION

after a photograph of Donald Hall at his home in Wilmot, NH

In the background are poplars. A blue sky
Jane would have walked under
with her dog

each morning
on their hike to the dew-damp hayfields
across Route 4. The grass neglected and shaggy,

she'd add red geraniums or the odd itinerant loon.
They'd sneak into poems the way
mold spots appear

in the bathtub
without anyone noticing. She'd find
skeletons in the pasture. Moccasins like black runes.

The dog would race its untroubled corridors.
Night would bring on cold fevers.
The bed slumped.

Modulating time,
the snow closed down the harvest
recitals. Geese strafed the highway lost

to ice. They headed south. Her hair
dribbled out. Medicinal syrups
smelled like chalk .

in the pantry.
A work of art in every whisper
or wheeze. He learned them all by heart.

He'd carry her when she couldn't walk.
She'd go slack—some primitive
reflex. Her ball

joints cracked
when she stretched. One day
the maple tree split in two. It had been

in good condition. His cat climbed it
religiously. Then it fell.
Top heavy,

prematurely old.
The wood decayed on the ground.
Soft as putty in the sockets. The trunk pointed

east/west across the yard. Horizontal
totem, splintered terminal
not ordained.

Hair grows,
even after death. A cut tulip unfurls
in a glass of water. The water rises into the air.

CHALLENGER

Tube of soundless particles.
Bullets of molten ice.
Residue of bravery,
violence self-imposed
not done upon, diffuse
in impure pigments of fire.
For reasons unknown to me,
it is something easy to believe.
Nobody really knows
its name. Its truth
is unfractionated though;
it is every bit the runaway
pollinator. Someone in a
passing car stopped
to give me the news.
Nothing would be the same.
A stranger promised me,
in a voice I had heard
before, *everything
will be alright.*

A TIME OF PLENTY

The echolalia of falling sleet
obscures the fire my feet
start in the grass. Last year's leaves

incarcerated in a crystal display
of ice. I have been breaking in
again. Flights of barn swallows

flash above oak trees, speckled
coliforms piercing the marbled
frame of dawn's radiograph.

The air tastes like damp cinder
and rain, like the mud-caked Holsteins
bumping muzzles in the yard,

the casement and lock softened
by dry rot, the bones of the window
cracking as they start, jiggle,

and rise like some barometer
moved by adolescent terror,
jerky and unsure of itself at first.

The shag inside is a new touch,
pooling like blood in the dark,
washing into and up the walls,

crowding the chewed moon
of a dartboard cleated chest high,
lending its current to the battery-

operated fish flopping an exaggerated
caudal fin back and forth
like a whisper of breeze

in the stillness of the room.
Knives to cut. Knives to dress.
Hooks and lines and lead.

Three deer heads bend into the blur,
their glass eyes glittering,
tiny mirrors slashed with oil.

What's left of the time it took
to dial the doctor on the rotary,
or grade the road's ragged limestone

without a flat, without leaving
the catalytic housing splintered
and squeaking like a weather vane.

Those years are deep-seated in me,
scattered to the winds, flotsam
of suppers and the profit

of age and labor—capsized in the spine
of a book that slips its anchor
and drops far down, off into the deep.

FIDDLERS

for Julien Fisera

Yelapa. The pizzicato of the fiddler
menacing with a pugilistic claw.
Gaslight eyes hover above his carapace
like scorched stars. Unspent foci fibrillate
inside the brittle calcium brain pan.
All night he paces the Saltillo tile
in his famine's march. At dawn,
the fishing boats are unmoored.
They ease from the lagoon,
slender prows slapping the water.
Fluted, lucent eels skitter behind
half-formed wakes. *Jasmin. Flor.*
All day the crabs rush past.
Doughboys out for blood and slaughter.
The dogs on the beach go at them
like lunatics. Seabirds pick apart the
mutilated remains. The unscathed try
to protect the useless corpses. They won't
leave until the dogs wander off.
The birds fill up and fly away down
the beach. The fiddlers wait for night.
The tide simmers darkly in. Then they come,
praising the dead with superficial
taps, coddling the loculated bodies,
plucking the empty skeletons of gas.

ENTRE RIOS

Born between rivers, you are infinitely
cultivated. Sand backwashed from the ocean.

Good silt down from the plains. Fermented
in Disneyworld bacteria, embryos fasciculate

in polluted foam. The water rises, wrapping
its chastity belt of syrup on the rocks.

Sunflowers feast in this grammar. Their words
are the river's when the birds rise, stiff at first,

then fluid. An afterthought brings one back,
mother low in her woven flight, double-checking

the nest. Fingers in the hourglass. Eggs
humming in their sleep. And the snake who lives

in every forest and field, under every bed,
far-seeing and ravenous, who'd eat

his own tail if it meant for one night
he was the shadow that silenced the rest.

BIRDS OF PARADISE

Cannibals whose will
transmits them from
one imaginary prison

to another, ancestral
buds multiplied by tribal
grafting; Paradise

raised them, but the earth
let them die. A soul
was a mistake

that was bound to happen.
I was raised on these
lessons. A refugee

in the right skin.
I shared everything
with nobody.

I suffered over the use
of the crying plyers,
the dirt under my nails,

rain with its vague
expectations. The dewy pupa
emerged below

my green wing and I
ignored it. I could not
bear its raw memory

or its name
passing between the bright
colors of my being.

I hate the children
of men. They show no
gratitude for muteness,

no sane defense of silence.
They live as mocked-up
nudes denuded

of their kindest selves.
It is time they practice
dying.

Nothing signifies
the heart's abstracted
grace as well.

TREE OF ONE

A shadow without scale or element
grows into a tree of one.
Its fieldrobber's roots fan out

in the fleshless earth. Mute brother
cut sturdier, fish bones tattooed

at the wrists. It fakes a limp.
It creaks in the wind. Its branches
curl like cauterized nematodes.

The train passes with great violence.
Its cyclops eye empties

the field's largess. The shadow

waits its turn, a goose with a crystal
to the slaughter.
Triggered, we watch it shrink,

the strange helix disintegrating.
It returns on guy wires,
casements splintered in the darkness,

propelled molecules of chaos,
back into the dark flow of consciousness.

FAMILIAR BANDAGES

When the Queen palm throws
its shadow on the folding table
and chairs, the tree doctor
climbs its pummeled fresco
the woodpeckers tunnel,
searching for answers, mining
disease. Bronze tomentum,
frond and fluff yanked to dregs,
scattered over the table—
a dusting of coal-black snow.
Cosmic sediment, galaxies
of slotted bugs, brittle pods
buffeted by fricatives of light.
Cells in a pool of plasma
writhing in tortured orgasm.
The dead fall to bits after climax.
Empty casings. Doppelganger shells.
The slopped scum of poison
scarved around the trunk
with a chip brush, familiar bandage
of stasis from suburban yards.
The nameless lady is ready
for war. She waits in no-man's-land,
testing the air, her spine's silver rings
sloshed with *fipronil*, ready-made
riot gear, fierce defender of the self,
her invisible nexus of history.

EASTER, EL SARGENTO

A train of cars in procession.
Going nowhere fast.
The wild goats in low cages,
wrestled into garrotes,
riding the school bus with the band.
Horns drifts over from the church.
The sea pitches forward.
Green chilies bump heads
in chocolate roux.
A policeman sells beer
from the trunk of his cruiser.
His partner spins a pistol.
The bomberos put up a cheer.
Everyone you love is at the table.
Boiled marrow coruscating,
fat and garlic, onion and salt.
A curtain of rain countersinks
divots in the dusty streets,
and for a minute even the old
men drop from hammocks
to dance to the tin birdsong.

LIFE GOES ON

*I am supposed to be an average
reasonable and intelligent young man.*

–Charles Joseph Whitman

I.

I am a person in a world of people.
The pen I use is rhythmic today,
scratching in the semi-dark.
I scribble a confession of useless
knots in measured obsidian.
I write about the mind that terrifies.
I never tire of turning that stone,
collecting the artifacts beneath.
It is an entry, like a street in a
medieval city whose occupants
choose who they murder and who
they let pass. It is not a vision only I
subscribe to. Life goes on,
they say, no matter what path
you're persuaded to try.
It fills you and you fill it
without knowing you do, making
of it an anonymous composite
of you—average, reasonable,
intelligent—to set sail or sink
like a captain with his ship.

II.

I am a person in a world of people.
Morale has become a mountainside.
The incline leads to a quick stream
that takes you down again.

My landscape is concrete and cement.
The engineers have run it smooth.
A half mile from here the view
will be a witness to the soul's

triumphant storm. Lost in the echo
of snow, pigeons gather in the yard.
A sentinel tower empties into the cold
estate ahead. Swallows rise beneath.

Hell will be blamed soon. No wolf
will greet you. An hourglass of bones,
a roadblock of coal. Let me push
the daisies from my hand,

slide the fever from my collar.
My palm is enormous. It spreads out
to take them in. It is an orchard
bleak and cruel. It is mine, not yours.

GIRL BURNING

The fatalists eat her for dinner.
They flip her inside out.
Esters of violence on the shortwave.
The hot flash of bloody mink.
The fire's tensile cavity swarms
her naked body. The soldiers
smell like mold, old dregs. They march
to no beat. One smokes a cigarette.
Another dreams of sand like sugar
in Alabama. She flaps down the road
of despair, dry sticks and flint.
The foreign sky comes to an end.
Smoke grazes the heavens and thins.
No touchable gold, no iron to wine,
the temples abandoned to beaks
and claws. A cloud of steam,
an eyebrow of sparks, what else
but the jaws of despair?

BOWL OF APPLES

Living has a certain ring to it. Dying just won't do.

    These green, perfect strangers impress on me

        the foolishness of rubbing shoulders

together in a still-life's shallow grave. They betray themselves

    in such a graceful way, auto-cannibals

        who expect to awaken in a universal

banquet, swollen in the juice of meaning. This is the kind

        of house I keep.

It is hard to imagine Houdini never escaping.

    I would like to say it would be painful to watch.

        These immortals here, the prize is in the leisure

of the picking. Maybe first. Maybe last. Never

            never crosses their minds. Their confinement

is prudence on my part. Without it, they all might roll away.

SENSE OF TIME

To you, a thread. To me, a plate
broken on the kitchen floor.
I'm shooing my daughters away.
Yelling at my wife across the room
to be careful, to avoid the sliver
that might slip into the exact
right crease in the sole of her foot
and take her away from us.

Whatever I say, my warning
will not be heeded. I will pick
some of it up by hand. Get out
the broom, the dustpan. The few
little shards I know are there but
can't be seen will have to be stepped
on to be found. I'll be listening
for that shout forever.

HOME SCHOOL

If I am to be as brilliant and as bold
as the many-forked map of the dogwood

whose creamy petals whisper
preternaturally from their leafy shelves,

there can be no early bloom or tender
distraction from the suffering it takes

to get there. Even as you pace
around the scribbled algorithms

on butcher paper, or squint beneath
the pale blinking sausages of the

lightbulbs overhead, there is nothing post-
mortem in your thought; everything

jumps to the front of the line:
looking for the speck of sand in the

oyster, searching the silky linings
of an old coat hanging in the closet.

You find a ticket inside before you know
what ticket means, or who put it there,

or why. Something no less human
has been here long before you,

moving the chairs into an Arthurian
circle, carving runes on the desktops,

asking similar questions to yours,
finding no satisfactory answers.

ACKNOWLEDGMENTS

The author would like to thank the editors of the following publications in which some of these poems first appeared, often in different form: *The Good Life Review*, The *Wells Street Journal*, *Analecta*, & *The Bangalore Review*. I must thank Thomas Whitbread (RIP) and David Wevill for sparking the fire, and Marvin Bell (RIP) for fanning it. And a very special thank you to my parents for their love and support.

ABOUT THE AUTHOR

REED SMITH was born in Weimar, Texas, in 1978. He graduated from The University of Texas and the Iowa Writers' Workshop. He has lived in many parts of the country, and has been a paramedic, a teacher, a geriatric advance care practitioner, and an actor who performed at The Globe, Orange Tree, and Swan Theatres in England. He lives in Hollywood, Florida, with his wife and twin daughters. This is his debut book of poems.

B A P
Brooklyn Arts Press

Brooklyn Arts Press (BAP) is an independent publishing house devoted to publishing books of poetry, novels, lyrical & short fiction, art & photography monographs, chapbooks, & nonfiction by emerging artists.

Visit us today at BrooklynArtsPress.com.

www.ingramcontent.com/pod-product-compliance
Lightning Source LLC
Chambersburg PA
CBHW060541080526
44586CB00012B/810